ANNIE BUFE LIPPE 1888-1992

ANNIE'S STORY

Memories of my Grandmother

Compiled by
Donna Gholson Cook

ABOOKS
Alive Book Publishing

Annie's Story
Copyright © 2017 by Donna Gholson Cook

Additional copies may be ordered from the publisher for educational,
business, promotional or premium use.
For information, contact ALIVE Book Publishing at:
alivebookpublishing.com, or call (925) 837-7303.

ISBN 13
978-1-63132-038-5

ISBN 10
1-63132-038-6

Library of Congress Control Number: 2017939468

Library of Congress Cataloging-in-Publication Data
is available upon request.

First Edition

Published in the United States of America by ALIVE Book Publishing
and ALIVE Publishing Group, imprints of Advanced Publishing LLC
3200 A Danville Blvd., Suite 204, Alamo, California 94507
alivebookpublishing.com

PRINTED IN THE UNITED STATES OF AMERICA

10   9   8   7   6   5   4   3   2   1

Dedicated to my grandsons,
Lucas Mitchell,
Dominic Legaspi,
and Brayden Legaspi

And to all of

Annie Lippe's Descendants,

100 and growing

CONTENTS

Acknowledgements   **9**
Preface   **11**

1. Crossing the Atlantic in the 1800s   **13**

2. Washington County, Texas   **17**

3. Moving West to Mills County   **19**

4. Love and Marriage of Annie and Fritz   **21**

5. Children and Farms   **25**

6. Farming the Land   **41**

7. Daily Life on the Farm   **49**

8. World Wars I and II   **63**

9. Church, School, Fun Times, Mischief   **67**

10. Illnesses, Accidents, Miraculous Escapes   **77**

11. Children leaving the Nest   **85**

12. Annie's Later Years   **91**

List of Children and Grandchildren   **99**

Acknowledgements

Many thanks to my wonderful aunts and uncles, Annie's children, who contributed stories and photos, and my mother, Annie's firstborn, Joe Ann, who left me a treasure of family photos. Also, thank you to Meta Mitchell, for a beautiful recollection of her "Aunt Annie."

A special thank you to my grandson, Dominic Legaspi, for his thoughtful editing. He gave me many excellent suggestions to make the story more interesting and understandable for today's young readers.

*****

For more stories and photos, see **Fritz and Annie Lippe Family, German Cotton Farmers in Early 1900s Texas**, Compiled and Edited by Donna Gholson Cook, available through major booksellers.

Preface

Excerpt from "My Aunt Annie"
by Meta Mitchell

I don't think I've ever known anyone more gentle, kind, and tenderhearted than Aunt Annie. I cannot recall ever seeing her angry. At the same time she was very strong and courageous, and endured many a hardship and heartache in her long life; as well as many happy and joyous times. I'm sure she would agree with me that it was her strong love and faith in God, and reliance on Him, that sustained her during her long life on this earth.

I think of her often during my own "walk of faith" and I just want to say in closing, this world would be a much better place if we had more "Aunt Annies!!"

Meta Mitchell

1. Crossing the Atlantic in the 1800s

Annie's mother, Sophie Schwartz, was fifteen years old in 1881 when she came to America from Germany with her mother, also named Sophie, along with a sister and two brothers. Their father had died of tuberculosis in Germany, and his desperate widow set out for America with their children. They came on a sailing ship and were on the Atlantic for months, some days going back about as many miles as they gained the day before. The living conditions on the ship were miserable. They must have been very relieved when they finally landed in Galveston, Texas, and a little apprehensive as they headed inland to find a place to settle, but Sophie was a brave woman.

Sophie Schwartz,
Annie Bufe Lippe's maternal grandmother.

Why would Sophie Schwartz and so many other Germans give up everything in their homeland to move to America? What would make the risk of crossing the ocean on a sailing ship worth the misery and danger? The trip was far from an enjoyable one. The conditions on the ships were almost unbearable, making the journey a long nightmare. The food was horrible until it ran out completely, and the drinking water was foul and smelly. The ships were terribly overcrowded, causing diseases to spread rapidly. Many people were seasick, and the smell of vomit was everywhere. The passengers who could not afford to travel first class were crammed into steerage with the cargo. Rats, bedbugs, and other pests spread disease and terror. Some passengers died and were buried at sea. When caught in a storm, the immigrants rightly feared that the ship would sink. Some ships went to the bottom with all aboard lost. Those who survived the journey were often so ill and weak when they arrived that they had to be carried off the ship.

The *Ben Nevis*.
One of the sailing ships carrying Germans to America in the 1800s.
About 5.5 million Germans came to America between 1814 and 1915.

How could life in Germany be so miserable that so many people were desperate to leave? Extreme poverty was a major reason for many. It was becoming harder and harder to make a living or even to survive by farming, and the only way to get land was by inheritance, so many people were unable to get land. Land in America was plentiful and available. Some people were in danger for speaking out against the government. Some were fleeing religious persecution, where if you were not of the "right" religion, you would be punished. Everyone was expected to conform to the beliefs of the ruler of their state, whether it was Catholic or Protestant. If they did not, they were persecuted as heretics. America held the promise of religious freedom. Another reason many left was to avoid the extremely harsh military training.

Annie's father, Gustave "Gus" Bufe was one of the latter. He left Germany just before he was drafted into the military because the training was so very cruel, strict and hard. His brother was drafted, and he drowned when he was forced to swim a river while training. That scared Gus so badly that he fled to America. He landed in New York about 1880 and stayed there until he paid off his debts to the people who paid for his voyage.

After about a year, he left New York for Texas. His daughter Annie said, "He had some more kinfolks here in Texas, so he traveled his way from New York, work a day, then have enough money to travel again for a day. That's the way he worked himself down here to Texas."

Gus and Sophie were both living in Washington County, about 100 miles inland from Galveston, when they met. They were **married in Brenham, Texas in 1886**, began farming cotton, and started their family of nine children. **Annie was their second child, born in 1888.** She had an older sister, Louise, six younger brothers, and one younger sister. The family was able to grow good crops in the fertile farmland of Washington County when the weather cooperated, until the boll weevil came to Texas.

Annie's parents, Gus and Sophie Schwartz Bufe,
after their marriage on January 2, 1886.

Gus and Sophie Bufe, many years later.

2. Washington County, Texas, before 1905

Gus and Sophie moved from farm to farm several times while they lived in Washington County. Annie's daughter Lena recalled hearing her say that her family lived in a log house near the Brazos River when she was young.

Brazos River, Washington County, looking north.

Gus liked farming the fertile river bottom land, but at times the Brazos River would flood and destroy their crops. Annie often told the story of the worst flood she experienced. The family had just finished sewing their sacks to start picking the cotton crop when a huge storm hit.

The rain began to fall around sunset and continued through the night. Gus boarded up the doors and windows and kept the barrels of sugar and flour dry by putting them under the table, which was covered by an oilcloth tablecloth. Gus and Sophie tied up their bedding and everything else and hung it from the ceiling. The terrified family huddled together in one corner and prayed as they waited for the long night to end. When the rain stopped at dawn and the sun rose, they looked out to see the damage. Their hearts sank when they saw that both their cotton and corn crops had been destroyed. Their income for the next year had been washed away, and they had to borrow money from relatives to live on until the next crop could be made. The six children in the family at the time ranged in age from infant to teenager. Annie was eleven, and was so shaken by the storm that she was terrified to even be near rivers and creeks for the rest of her life.

It was not the weather but the invasion of the boll weevil that did what the floods failed to do--drive many farmers out of Washington County. Cotton grows as a soft fiber in a protective case called a "boll" around the seeds of the plant. The weevils ate the cotton buds and flowers, totally destroying the cotton. Some neighbors were moving west to Mills County, Texas, so Gus and Sophie decided to do the same. The growing German population and good farmland made Mills County appealing, and the boll weevil had not yet spread that far west.

3. Moving West to Mills County

Annie was seventeen when her family moved from Washington County to Mills County. She remembered the move very well and often told the story to her children and grandchildren.

In the winter of 1905, her mother was very close to giving birth to her eighth child, Annie's younger brother Oscar. Gus and Sophie's family moved with all of their belongings by train. When they arrived, the house they were going to rent was not ready for them. The only thing available was a very small house that they would have to stay in temporarily.

Try to imagine the large family, with everything they owned, in an unheated two-room house, in the middle of winter, stumbling over all of the contents of their previous house and barn, without food or firewood. They were in the tiny house for over a month, miserably waiting for the house they were going to rent to become vacant.

One friendly family who owned a store in the town of Priddy found out about the family's situation and asked for some help in milking their herd of ten or eleven cows. Annie would get up early and go out in the cold winter weather every morning to help them, and in return she was able to take some of the milk to her own family.

When the family moved to Mills County, it was too soon to butcher their hogs, so they left them with Annie's older sister Louise and her husband in Washington County. Louise and her husband butchered the hogs when the weather was cold enough, packed the meat in boxes with salt, and sent the boxes to Annie's family by train. Before refrigeration was available, salt was used to preserve pork for a short time. When the boxes arrived, they were added to the already crowded two-room house. In Annie's words,

> We had everything in the house, you might say. All we used to have outside in barns, harness and everything else for the horses, that house was just so stuffed full, you couldn't even get through hardly, but

we had to stay there until the house was ready to
move in. – *Annie Bufe Lippe*

Not being familiar with this new area, Gus did not know
where to get anything, even firewood, so another friendly neighbor
showed him around and helped him in every way he could. The
firewood was not only needed for heat, but the boxes of pork could
only be kept for about a week without spoiling and had to be
preserved longer by being smoked.

The month they spent stuffed into that tiny house with
everything they owned must have seemed very long to the Bufe
family.

4. Love and Marriage of Annie and Fritz

Annie's family had been living in Mills County for several years when she met Fritz Lippe. Fritz was fourth in a family of twelve children. When he was eleven years old, his father, Henry, suffered permanent brain damage as the result of a heat stroke. He was a patient in a state hospital in Austin when he disappeared about 1900 and was never seen again. Fritz's mother, Louise, continued farming and raising her family alone. Tragically, two of her small daughters died very young. She moved her family to Mills County about the same time that Annie's family moved. The families knew each other in Washington County but lost contact in Mills County because they went to different churches.

Fritz's family, about 1902. Fritz is on the right, standing.
Their mother, Louise Lippe, is seated in the center.

Annie was at a community picnic when she noticed Fritz for the first time. She saw him looking at her with his blue eyes, and then he invited her to ride on a hobby horse (carousel), a special treat. After the first ride, he asked her if she would like another one,

and she accepted. Then he offered to buy her some ice cream, and
she accepted that, too.   After that, they were boyfriend and
girlfriend.

Fritz Lippe as a young man.

Fritz and Annie dated for more than a year before they
started planning their wedding. Annie's father owed money on his
farm, so he offered to make a deal. If they wanted to get married
right away, they would just have to go to church and get married
without a big celebration. If they were willing to wait another year,
he would be able to afford to give them a big wedding.

The next time Fritz came over, Annie told him of her father's
offer. His answer was, "That's fine with me. Then I can work
another year and make enough money so we can buy a team." With
their own team of two horses, Fritz and Annie could begin farming
and having children. Fritz worked another year, living with his
mother and earning fifty cents a day, breaking new ground all that
winter. It was an exhausting job. This was before tractors were

available, so he had to dig into hard ground, following a plow behind a team of horses.

Annie and Fritz were married on December 8, 1910, and the invitations were delivered in a most unusual way. Several boys were chosen to ride to as many houses as possible in a day on nice ponies, all brushed and shiny. As each pony arrived at the first house, the invitation was accepted by tying a big bow on the saddle horn. At the next house, another bow was added somewhere else on the pony, and by the time they were finished at the end of the day, the horses were covered with bows from head to toe! Annie said that there was a lot of whooping and hollering as they rode back in!

Their wedding was in the church Annie's family attended, and the reception was at Annie's parents' house. She said that there were so many wagons and people, it seemed that everyone in Mills County was there. Many tables were set up in the house, but there were not nearly enough. The whole yard was full, and the men were getting hungry before the meal was ready, so they started a bonfire outside and started cooking sausages.

Annie remembered it as one of the happiest days in her life. She said that the weather was cold, but nice. Her younger brother Bill was about three years old at the time, and he held tightly onto her dress because he did not want to lose her. He was very fond of his big sister. In less than a year, the little boy would become an uncle!

Annie and Fritz Lippe, a few days after their wedding.

5. Children and Farms

1911-1912

Fritz and Annie's first year of marriage was spent living on a farm very close to their church and the pastor's family, the **Kunkel farm**. Annie had happy memories of the pastor's family. They were close friends, and the pastor's children were very hard workers. Annie said,

> We were close neighbors the first two years, really close neighbors, and we sure did neighbor, too, and the children worked in the fields for us, these little pastor's children. They were happy-go-lucky when they came to our field and we'd all get out there in the field, maybe in the evenings we could sing pretty good, and all those little pastor's children, they could sing, and the more we could sing, the better we could pick cotton. – *Annie Lippe*

When the pastor's wife made a trip to Germany, Annie had a chance to practice being a mother. She said, "That older little girl came running through that little pasture every once in a while, 'Can you help me out with this? I don't know how to do it.'" Annie said, "At that time, I wasn't much of a mother, either, but I did help out all I could."

Annie's first child, **Joe Ann, was born on October 29, 1911,** while they lived on this farm. Joe Ann was the first of twelve children--eight girls and four boys. One daughter died soon after birth. Annie's young brother Bill (the one who hung onto her wedding dress) said that he went to stay with his sister to babysit Joe Ann. He was only four, and it was not long before he became homesick. He was very glad to see the buggy coming to get him.

1912-1921

After renting for the first year, Fritz and Annie were able to start buying a farm of their own. They called this the **Washboard**

Farm because it was near Washboard Creek, named for the shape of the rocks in the river bed. One big rain storm raised the level of the creek almost to the house, so Fritz decided to move it farther from the creek. Somehow, they raised up the house and moved it.

Four more children were born at the Washboard Farm— **Lydia on February 16, 1916**; **John on June 29, 1917**; a daughter named **Annie on April 20, 1919**, who died shortly after she was born; and a son named **Fritz on March 18, 1920**.

Joe Ann, Lydia, and John, about 1920.

1921-1922

After nine years on the Washboard farm, Papa Fritz saw an enticing advertisement for land in Atascosa County, south of San Antonio. He sold the Washboard farm and **bought 100 acres near Charlotte.** That turned out to be a huge mistake. It was impossible to make a living farming the hot desert sand. As they were moving in, the family on the next farm was moving out. Many had already gone. To make matters worse, Fritz's mental health was deteriorating, and he often spent much time alone in the pasture. During this trying time, Annie gave birth to their sixth child (the fifth of those who survived), **Velma, born September 17, 1921**. All of Annie's babies were born at home, usually without the help of a doctor. When it was time for Velma to be born, a neighbor came to the house to help. Annie said that the neighbor, Mrs. Stussy, saved her life and Velma's.

By that time, Fritz was not carrying his share of the workload with the farm and family. Annie was overwhelmed, trying to farm and take care of six children, from infant to age ten. When her parents learned about her situation, they sent their pastor and a relative down to talk Fritz into moving back to Mills County. He finally gave in, and they moved back by train, livestock and all. Baby Velma cried from hunger all the way back on the train. When they arrived at Annie's parents' home, starving and exhausted, there was a huge meal waiting for them. Annie was so very happy to be home.

1922-1930

The next eight years were spent on the **Schuster farm** near Priddy. It was one of the children's favorite farms, and they had many fond memories of living there. Annie was again surrounded by loving family and friends. Four more children were added to the family--**Martha, born September 21, 1923; Ben, born March 13, 1925; Lena, born October 12, 1926; and Martin, born February 25, 1929**.

Velma had wonderful memories of the Schuster farm. She recalled,

> I lived on the Tony Schuster place about eight years, and those years were spent with pleasure, because it was a beautiful place to live. In summer all the trees were pretty and green, and many Sunday afternoons were spent by playing under those trees with dolls, and school, and many other games with my brothers and sisters. We would see a very pretty

sunset most every night which was more pretty than words can tell.

Riding the old horse Roan was great fun also. Hunting grapes and berries was a great pleasure to do with my cousins trying to see which one could get the most.

My parents sure did hate to think about moving away from there but the land was too poor to make our living so we rented a place from Fritz Stegemoller. – *Velma Lippe Bretting*

Joe Ann holding sister Velma and cousin Frances Roark,
Schuster farm, about 1922.

Cousin "Tuffy" Bufe, John, Fritz, Lydia, and Joe Ann holding Velma,
on the same day as the previous photo.

Velma, Ben, Martin, Lena, Martha, Schuster farm, about 1929.

Windmill and field, Schuster farm, 1978.

Old barn still standing at the Schuster farm in 1978!
Lydia, Annie, and John.

1930-1935

For the next five years, the family lived on the **Stegemoller farm** near Indian Gap in Hamilton County, Texas. The farm house was still standing in the 1980s. Two of the boys, John and Fritz, slept on the porch, even in winter. The two youngest children were born during this time, **Katie on May 4, 1930, and Ruth on September 16, 1931**.

Stegemoller Farm House in 1977.
Katie and Ruth were born in this house.
Children were usually born at home, with no doctor present.

Stegemoller Farm House, 1980s.

The house does not look big enough for a family of thirteen, but back in those days there were usually three family members sleeping in a full size bed. The children went to school in Indian Gap, riding in a buggy pulled by their horse Roan, sometimes in ice

and snow.   One time, Roan was running too fast and wound up
sliding and hurting himself, and breaking the buggy.   Lena
remembered going to Indian Gap school with the horse and buggy,
and how the lap robe, a blanket that they spread over their legs and
tucked under them, kept them warm on very cold days.   The school
group photo below includes five of the Lippe children, Fritz, Velma,
Martha, Lena, and Benjamin.   Notice that all of the children whose
feet are visible are barefoot.

Indian Gap school students and teachers, 1933.

TOP ROW LEFT TO RIGHT
5TH ₹ 6TH GRADE TEACHER
ALVIN PETE SEIDER -+
BETTY HIT
FRITZ LIPPE
ROSIE NAVERT
O V BURKES
RILEY MITCHELL
CLOE SARGENT
WADE BRANHAM
FLORA MARWITZ
ERMA SEIDER
JW GRIFFIS
EMMA SEIDER
VELMA LIPPE
WALTER REINHARDT
DUB HARRIS
? ?

BOTTOM ROW
BOBBY RICHARDSON
BECKY MITCHELL
WAYLAND HOWINGTON
WARREN BRANHAM
CHARLES DAVIDSON
GERTRUDE STEGOMOELLER
CONA MARWITZ

2ND ROW L-R
MILFORD ROBERTS
ALVIN HIT
DUB HARRIS
ALVIN STEGOMOELLER
? ?
GLEN BYNUM
GILBERT NEWSOM
DOLE BYNUM
? ROBERTS
WILLIE MARWITZ
NIG TOLLIE
PV OWEN
LOYD HIT
RAYMOND MARWITZ
MARTHA LIPPE
DORIS HEDGEPATH
ROBERT L. HOWERTH

IMOGENE BROWN

AWTWMN
1933
INDIAN GAP

3RD ROW L-R
WJ MAYFIELD
JUANITA BOLTEN
LENA LIPPE
TJ BURKES
SUE MITCHELL
? ?
SYLVIA ?
JAMES HARRIS
WALLACE HOWINGTON
WALTER NAVERT
HILDA MAYFIELD
MEXICAN JOE
AUBERY ROBERTS
? ?
NOEL BYNUM
? ?
BENJAMIN LIPPE

TEACHERS
MERLYN GOOCH
RUTH HILL

Top Row teacher
INA JO WALTON

Names of students and teachers in photo 5.9.

Abandoned Indian Gap school building, still standing in 2008.

1935-1938

The next three years were spent on the **Charlie Tiemann place**, back in the Priddy area. By the time Fritz and Annie moved to the Tiemann farm, the older children were beginning to leave home and find jobs. Velma said that when they moved to this farm, they had to fight Johnson grass until they had blisters on their hands. Johnson grass is a troublesome weed that is almost impossible to get rid of. Its sharp edges cut into hands and destroy surrounding plants. The Lippes were always moving near someone who had Johnson grass that needed pulling, and their dad sent the kids to pull it in trade for something or to earn some money for the family. They were too tired to have any fun after they finished doing the supper dishes.

Fritz and Annie celebrated their 25th wedding anniversary on this farm. The children gave them a big surprise party. Joe Ann and Lydia, who were working away from home, came home to do all of the cleaning and getting everything ready for the party. Joe Ann had to leave to go back to work before the family photo was taken.

Fritz and Annie, 25th anniversary. Left to right: Martin, Ben, Fritz (son), John, Fritz (father), Annie, Lydia, Velma, Martha, Lena, Katie, Ruth.

Fritz and Annie, 25th anniversary,
Tiemann place, with many friends and relatives.

1938-1941
For the next three years, the family lived on the **Bryant farm** near Pottsville, Hamilton County. Like the Schuster place, the Bryant farm was a beautiful place to live. Unfortunately, they had to move because of health problems.

Bryant farm. Ruth, Martin, Katie, Lena, Annie, and Fritz near the barn.

Bryant farm, 1939. Fritz, Velma, Joe Ann, Martha, and John.

1941-1942

In January 1941, Fritz and Annie moved to the **Charlie Meyer farm** near Veribest, near San Angelo, in Tom Green County because of the family's asthma problems. Annie said, "That doctor told us to move up to a little higher climate and we moved up toward San Angelo." They lived on the Meyer farm for only one year. Only five of their eleven children were still at home when they moved to Veribest.

1942-1952

Their last farm was the **Niemann farm** near Veribest. The farm house had two stories, with one finished room at the top and an unfinished area where the boys slept. They could see the shingles on the roof above their heads from their beds. If it snowed during the night, they would awaken in the morning with snowflakes on their covers. They once had a goldfish in a bowl and the water froze solid during the night. Someone put the bowl beside the stove to thaw and the goldfish actually revived and lived for a while, although Martin said that the fish never seemed quite the same after that.

Niemann farm, 1940s. Ben, Lena, Katie, and Ruth,
tired after hoeing cotton all day. The dog's name was Scottie.

Lippe family, Niemann farm, 1940s. Back row: Katie, Ruth, Martha;
Middle: Ben, Joe Ann, Lena, Fritz, Velma, John;
Front: Annie, Papa Fritz, Martin, Lydia.

Niemann farm, Christmas 1950.
Four Brothers: Martin, Fritz, John, Ben.

San Angelo park, 1940s.
Seven Sisters: Martha, Lena, Ruth, Velma, Joe Ann, Katie, Lydia.

Ruth, Katie, and Lena, having fun riding around with a neighbor,
Elenora Hohertz, on a Sunday afternoon in 1948.

Ruth remembered her mother buying their first refrigerator when they lived on the Niemann farm.

> We got the electric refrigerator in the late forties. The brand was International Harvester.

Martin may remember the year we got it. I remember a couple of salesmen came to the farm at the Niemann place near Veribest selling refrigerators. Mama didn't want to buy it. She said we couldn't afford it. The guys said, "We will leave it with you for a couple of weeks. If you don't like it, we will take it back to the store." When they came back, of course Mama didn't want to part with it so we made arrangements to buy it. Yes, we had an ice box before that. I can't remember if we bought ice blocks in Veribest or if someone brought the ice to the house. I know we had to keep a pan under the ice box to catch the melting ice. We had to empty it at least every day. Sometimes we would forget and have to mop up water when the pan would run over. – *Ruth Lippe Atkins Cleckler*

Most of the children grew up and left the nest during the ten years on the Niemann farm. Annie was still farming the Niemann place with son Martin, age nineteen, and daughter Ruth, seventeen, in 1952. After a couple of years of drought and a very small crop, she decided to move to Odessa. Annie's story after moving into town will continue in Chapter 11. First, though, let us learn more about what life was like on the Lippes' farms.

6. Farming the Land

Who owned the land?

Landowners often rented portions of their land to farming families to raise crops, allowing the family to live in a house on the property. The renters were called *tenant farmers*. Before tractors, the work was done manually or with horses, and the job was too big for the landowner to do it without help. The size of the Lippe family farms averaged 160 acres, all over 100 acres. The Niemann farm was the largest at 190 acres. Martin said that all of the farms except Washboard and the one at Charlotte were rented, usually giving the landowner 1/4 of the cotton receipts and 1/3 of the grain receipts as payment for use of the land.

When tractors became available, the landowners were able to farm their own land, and they often evicted the tenants who had been living on the property and farming the land for years. That was understandably the cause of many hard feelings on the part of the tenants.

Son Fritz on family's first tractor. Meyer farm, 1941.

What crops were grown?

Cotton was the main cash crop grown by the Lippe family, but they also grew corn, wheat and oats to feed to the livestock and sell if they had an excess. Velma remembered, "When we had a good crop we were in the field early to late. At times we were barefoot. That dirt sure was hot." A large garden supplied fresh vegetables in the summer, with some being canned or stored in the cellar for the winter.

Velma, Ruth, and Ben, working in the field about 1942.

What animals did they have?

Before the advent of tractors and other farm machinery, animals were very important to survival on a farm for getting the work done and for providing food. All of the farming was done with a team of horses until the Lippes moved to Veribest, where they bought their first tractor. On average, they had about four horses, as some were more suited to plowing, and others were better at pulling a wagon. Chickens were an important source of eggs and meat. The family raised hogs for meat and byproducts, rendering the fat to make lye soap for laundry and other uses. They also had four or five milk cows for milk, cream, and butter, and their calves, which were sold.

What were the jobs of family members?

It is hard for us to understand the amount of work it took to grow or make almost everything needed for a family of thirteen to survive, with our modern conveniences everywhere we turn. Annie would talk about how, after working all day, she would start making clothes for the children and cutting out quilt blocks until late at night. She baked bread twice a week, from scratch, which was quite a job, kneading the dough and letting it rise.

Ruth gave the following description of the work done by every member of the family, starting at about age five!

When it was chopping and picking cotton season, the days got very long working in the fields. Before we would go to the field in the morning we would do the morning chores and help Mama with breakfast. We always ate a big breakfast.

We would start working about sun up and work till sun down. We did take a couple hours break for dinner, the noon meal. For us to know when it was noon, Mama would throw a white towel on the roof of the house. We knew it was time for us to go to the house for dinner. We could see the house from the field. Of course we didn't have clocks or watches in the field. We sure didn't have cell phones. We sure looked for that towel so we could take a break for dinner. We also took a lunch for a short afternoon break. We would sit in the shade of the wagon. The wagon was in the field for us to empty our cotton sacks into when it was picking or pulling cotton time. We had a cotton scale to weigh our cotton each time we got our sacks full. I (Ruth) would pick about 150 lbs. a day but my sisters and brothers would get two to three hundred lbs. a day. We got paid ten cents for every hundred lbs. we picked. Maybe the older sisters and brothers got a little more. I don't remember for sure.

Water was kept in gallon jugs wrapped with heavy cloth or toesack (gunnysack) material. We would wet the cloth to keep the water cool.

Mama would sew our cotton sacks out of ducking material *(a heavy, plain woven cotton fabric, similar to the material in sneakers and tents)*. Mama also sewed knee patches on our overalls so when our backs would hurt too bad from bending over picking cotton we would get on our knees and crawl to give our backs a rest.

After our break in the afternoon we would start watching the sun. Anxious for it to go down so we could go home. However our work wasn't over yet. We would go to the house and do the evening chores like milking the cows, feeding pigs and chickens, gathering the eggs, etc. Some of us would help Mama with supper. The girls always cleaned the kitchen after supper. We were ready for bed after that. That was pretty much our day on the farm in the summer time.

We did get to go home from the fields a little early on Saturday so we could take a bath, help Mama with washing clothes, and study our Sunday school lessons. Sunday we always went to Sunday School and church. We had the whole afternoon off. A day of rest and worship, the Lords day.

I worked hard on the farm at Veribest chopping, picking, and pulling cotton. Also working with grain and livestock. My sisters, brothers, and I had to miss a lot of school because of farm work. – *Ruth Lippe Atkins Cleckler*

Lippe family members picking cotton. They covered their skin as much as possible to keep from getting a tan, which would identify them as manual laborers. Often only their hands were tan, as can be seen in many photos in this book.

Ruth picking cotton at the Niemann farm, 1940s.

Lippe family member picking cotton. Notice the bulging cotton sack pulled behind the worker. The white cotton bolls can be seen on the plants not yet picked.

How did weather affect farming?

Farming is always a gamble, because weather is always a factor in the success or failure of the year's crops. Just as the flooding Brazos River in Washington County destroyed the crops when Annie was a child, weather often varies in many ways--too much rain, too little rain, rain at the wrong time, hailstorms, early or late freezes--all of these can be devastating to the income that the family is depending upon to survive another year. That is just as true for farmers today as it was in the early 1900s.

Martin remembered a storm that came up while he was working in the field of the Niemann farm near Veribest. His granddaughter Sarah, age eleven at the time, asked him to tell his story of a storm for one of her school projects. Sarah wrote,

Around May or June of 1948 Martin Lippe was working in a cotton field. It was around 2:00 p.m. and he had been planting cotton for 6 or 7 hours now. When he looked up he saw this big black cloud coming toward him, so he was worried. Martin was 18 and lived on a farm in West Texas. He went to go round up the cows, to put them in the barn. In came the cloud shortly. Martin, his sister Ruth, and their Mom went to their house. When they got inside it started to hail. The storm came from the northwest so when they were in the west room they couldn't hear each other but they could see the other person's lips moving. They were worried that the storm would blow the west room away so they moved to the east room.

After about 45 min. the storm was over, it rained 6 inches. There was a lot of damage: broken windows, roofs coming apart, mud in the house. Martin had to shovel the mud out of the house. When Martin went to check on the car he couldn't get the door open to check on the car, because there was so much hail. Then Martin went to check on the cows. When he got to the barn, they weren't there, then he saw fences knocked down, they were in the field. He was happy about that. When Ruth and Martin were done checking on the cotton field they told their Mom that the cotton plants were smashed to the ground and that the hail was about an inch big.

After talking to friends the Lippes found out that their farm was one of the worst damage wise.

After planting the crops, putting on a new roof, putting in new windows, putting up new fences, and more, a month later everything was back to normal.

About 48 years later Martin has never seen that bad of a hail storm since.

By Sarah Lippe, age 11

7. Daily Life on the Farm

What did they eat, and where did they get it?

It was quite a challenge to supply enough food for a hardworking family of two adults and eleven growing children. Meals were often the same from day to day, depending upon the season, and the quantity of food was barely enough. Most food was raised on the farm, and only a few items, such as flour, sugar, and coffee, were bought with money from the sale of the annual cotton crop. When asked about the food they ate, Velma shared some of her memories.

> We always had a big garden. Planted lot of potatoes to last about till the next spring. These were stored in the dirt cellar. We did a lot of canning. One year Dad went to a peach orchard in the wagon and bought 10 bushels of peaches to be canned. Neighbors came over to help peel peaches. We sat in the kitchen for several days, I think, peeling them. Killed a rooster for dinner--were in a beef club. *(Before refrigerators, farm families would take turns butchering a steer and sharing the meat with other families in the club.)* We had sweet rice, peaches, potatoes often. Good fresh light bread with home churned butter. Post Toasties for birthdays. Turning the ice cream freezer. – *Velma Lippe Bretting*

Martha recalled...

> ...About raising a vegetable garden in the spring and summer. I'm sure some of the things we grew would be potatoes, carrots, green beans, peas, and tomatoes. I think we did can some green beans sometimes, maybe it depended on how good the crop was. Also, we may have raised and canned some black-eyed

peas sometimes too. We would store the potatoes in
a cool place like a cellar, where they wouldn't freeze.

Fruits, especially peaches--we usually canned
lots of peaches, as we all liked the home canned
peaches. Peaches with mashed potatoes was one of
our basic meals. At times I think we also canned
some pears and apricots. I don't recall anything about
canning tomatoes, which I suppose would go in the
vegetable group. On rare occasions I think we would
plant some watermelon and cantaloupe too. Also, I'm
sure we raised pinto beans which would have to be
dried when harvested. I recall quite frequently
having a meal of pinto beans and cornbread. –
Martha Lippe Hosum

Annie working in her garden, Meyer farm, about 1941.

Martin remembered the bread his mother baked. She usually
used corn meal with flour. Then if they had company, she would
just use flour. They hated that and were glad when that bread was
gone. They would sort the corn and keep the good ears to be ground
for corn meal, to use for bread.

Lena said, "When Dad took cotton to the gin, sometimes he would bring us back some apples. How good they were out in the hot field."

Annie, like many other farm wives, took good care of her flock of chickens, a good source of food, but she once said in an interview that the family was often hungry. Sometimes they had molasses, smoked ham and oatmeal. On Sundays they usually had rice soaked in water and then cooked in milk with sugar.

Annie was proud of the eggs laid by her hens.

Annie with son Fritz, home on leave during World War II.

How did they cook and heat the house? Did they have lights?

Have you ever had the the power go out in your neighborhood? No lights, no radio, no television, the microwave is dead. So you scrounge around to find a flashlight with batteries that are still working, just to be able to find your pajamas and crawl into bed, hoping that the power will come back on by morning. What did the Lippe family do before electricity or gas? Katie said, "We burned coal in the stoves on the farm. Maybe some wood." To see at night, they used kerosene lamps, according to Martin. He said that they got electricity about 1948 and a telephone around 1939, when he was about ten. How you can have a phone without electricity? Back in those days, before satellites and cell phone towers, all telephones were land lines, attached to the wall with a cord. Many people still have them, because they may be the only phones working in times of emergency. They can operate without electricity, because there is a small amount of current carried through the phone line. When the Lippe family got their first phone, several families shared a party line. Each house had an individual ring, making it possible for neighbors to pick up their receiver and listen to the conversation if they were bored or nosy.

What did they wear? How did they do laundry?

Clothes for most boys were overalls or rompers and jeans for the men, while all females wore dresses made out of feed sacks. Some items bought in large quantities, such as flour, sugar, and chicken feed, were sold in bags made of a sturdy printed cloth material. Farm wives were very glad to get it and used it to sew clothes for their children and themselves.

For doing the laundry, they made their own soap, as Martin recalled.

> Clothing was washed with homemade lye soap, one of the byproducts of the annual slaughter of hogs. Solids remaining after rendering lard, as well as rinds from hams, were boiled for a long time until all scraps were dissolved. It was necessary to keep stirring, so that the solids did not stick to the bottom of the pot. – *Martin Lippe*

Lye was made from ashes collected from wood stoves. When they were ready to make the soap, they poured water through the ashes and skimmed off the extremely caustic liquid lye. Making soap was a very dangerous process. If someone made a mistake, there was a good chance of inhaling poisonous fumes or being severely burned.

On wash day, a fire was built under a big iron pot to heat the water, which was carried in buckets to fill the tub for the washboard, and later the washing machine. More tubs were used for rinsing, and the rinse water was used to water the flowers. Clothes were hung on a clothesline to dry.

Washboard and tub similiar to Annie's. Clothes were scrubbed clean by hand
on the rippled area of the board. The same tub was used for family baths.

With no indoor plumbing, what did they do for baths and toilets?

What??? No water in the house? No bathrooms? How was
that possible? What on earth did they do? None of the Lippe farm
houses had indoor plumbing or bathrooms. Water needed in the
house came from underground. A well was dug, and a windmill
powered a pump to bring water to the surface. Any water needed
for cooking, washing dishes, or bathing had to be carried from the
well into the house in buckets.

Stegemoller farm, 1980s. Notice the windmill and tank.

For a toilet, they would dig a hole in the ground, about 50 to 150 feet from the house, making sure that it was downhill from the water well to avoid contamination of the water supply. A small wooden building was placed over the hole, with a wooden bench inside against the back wall. A hole was cut in the middle of the bench for them to sit on, or sometimes two holes--a larger one for grownups and a smaller one for children. The pages of an outdated Sears, Roebuck & Co. catalog were used for toilet paper, then corn cobs when the catalog ran out. Ouch! There may have been wasps, spiders, or snakes inside, and it was a good idea to rattle a stick around in the hole before sitting down! Going to the bathroom was uncomfortable and dangerous. When the hole in the ground was full, the outhouse was moved to a newly dug hole, and the old one was covered with dirt.

One example of an outhouse.
They did not always have such a fancy seat!

The family members took baths only once a week, on
Saturday, and the clothes that were worn all week were washed also.
Of course, there was no such thing as deodorant.   Martha
remembered bath times.

> Mama would put some warm water in a large
> round tub and at least two or three of us children
> would bathe in the same water before dumping it out
> and getting clean water.   Don't remember if we
> argued about who would be the first to go into the
> clean water but we did all get our baths on Saturdays,
> probably while Mama was busy making the coffee
> cakes for our Sunday morning breakfast. – *Martha
> Lippe Hosum*

Lena added,

> Also at this time baths in the galvanized tub
> would begin, heating water on the stove in the
> kitchen. With no bath room, doors were closed, and

we took our turn, not always getting clean water for each person. – *Lena Lippe Teinert*

Where did they buy necessary items that they could not make or grow?

There were few stores within range of a buggy ride, but almost everything imaginable could be ordered from the Sears, Roebuck & Co. catalog. A farmer could buy buggies for around $50, farm tools, animal supplies, windmills, and musical instruments. An organ similar to the one owned by the Lippe family was priced at $27.45 in the 1902 catalog. People could order clothing or cloth to sew, wood burning stoves, furniture, and household goods. The Sears catalog was the Amazon.com of the day, but the delivery time was a lot longer!

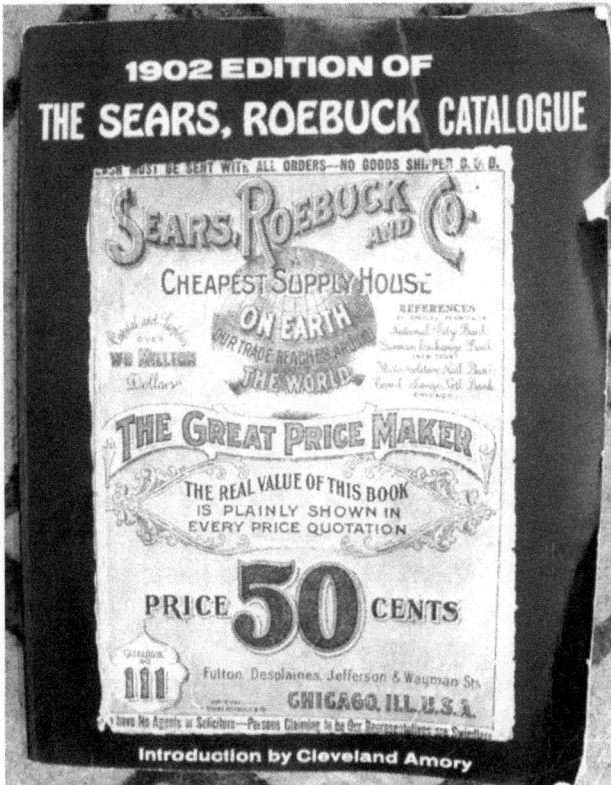

1902 Edition of The Sears, Roebuck and Co. Catalogue (replica)

How did they travel?

Joe Ann with uncles Oscar and Bill Bufe, about 1916.
Notice the buggies in the background.

Before cars, the most common way to travel was by a horse drawn buggy or wagon. A buggy has one seat, but might hold as many as two adults and three children. At one time, they were a two-buggy family. A hack was a two-seater buggy, but for large families like the Lippe family, they could all jump onto a wagon pulled by a team of horses. Annie talked about the condition of the roads used by wagons.

It was black dirt, and what I mean that was muddy when it rained...they were just common little roads, you might say, like through a field, and such as that.

And then when you had to travel, maybe with a wagon, you had little old paddles to clean your wagon wheels often. They would clog up, clog up, so much that you couldn't roll any more. – *Annie Lippe*

A friend, Anna Hohertz.
Car wheels got muddy, too, before roads were paved!

Annie remembered well the first time she saw (or didn't see) an automobile, when she was visiting her aunt in Washington County.

We was all out there close to the road, working in the garden. What is that? Zoom--it was by. That was an automobile, what you called, running on wheels, they

said. No, that went so quick, we didn't even get a
glance at it. – *Annie Lippe*

Annie never drove an automobile, but she could ride a horse
and drive a wagon. She remembered the first airplane she had ever
seen, because it landed in their own field! During the 1920s,
barnstormers, pilots with small planes, went from place to place
selling rides or performing stunts for the local population, most of
whom had probably never seen an airplane before. Annie recalled,

> We had a picnic over there, just right close to where
> we was living across the road, a three-day picnic.
> That little bitty old plane, he landed in our stubble
> field, where we had oats on. He gave people rides.
> He'd pick them up and circle around the picnic
> ground for a dollar. – *Annie Lippe*

Lydia was one of those who got a free ride because the pilot
had the use of their field. She said that she must have been about
eight. Unfortunately, at the next farm, the plane crashed and the
pilot died. Annie told Lydia, "It was the next place where he was
going to give people rides that the guy crashed. You all were pretty
lucky that you all didn't end up in a stubble field head over heel."
Annie said that she made it through her life without flying in an
airplane.

How did they hear news of the world?

History teacher John Franklin interviewed Annie for his
classes and asked her if she remembered hearing about the first
flight of the Wright brothers. She did not recall hearing anything
about that, but she did remember hearing about the sinking of the
Titanic during the first year that she was married. Annie said,

> We usually didn't have a newspaper, but our pastor
> did, and he was from South Dakota, and he always
> had his paper from his home town. Boy, he came
> over there to us and said, "Have you all heard? I want

to read something to you." And that ship went down, and boy, that was the first shock that I really remember we had after we got married, that that ship went down...We didn't have no magazine, no paper, nothing in our house, you might say. It was pretty bare in our house the first few years. – *Annie Lippe*

They usually heard about important world events on Sunday morning at church. They were living on the Washboard farm when they heard about the beginning of World War I. Annie said,

> That first World War, we had our church picnic out in the pasture, that's when somebody came up and brought us that news. That's what I remember when that first World War broke out and they said right away, "Now Germany's going to be really in some big trouble." – *Annie Lippe*

8. World Wars I and II

Treatment of Germans

World War I was not only trouble for Germany, as Annie predicted, but also for Americans of German descent. Her father, Gus Bufe, and many others, had not finalized their citizenship papers, which gave them quite a scare when they were accused of being spies. Annie recalled about her father's experience,

> ... one would think that making all those trips to Goldthwaite they would have really picked him up. No, they came out there to the field and really talked to him, taking his pictures and everything. They naturally thought he was a spy because he wasn't a citizen yet. Boy at that time, Germans that were here, they really were strict against them. They finally got it worked out that he had his papers all fixed up and he was a citizen. They charged those people in the first world war if they didn't have their papers, for sure... On my daddy, that was pretty rough, I'll tell you right now. They came out there and tried to talk to him and said since he wasn't a citizen, he was a spy and it was pretty hard stuff to look at. – *Annie Lippe*

Martin said that the neighbors assured the government officials that Gus was just a farmer trying to support his family, but they still took his picture and fingerprints in the field where he was working.

Annie recalled another scare experienced by their pastor during the war.

> Pastor Becker, he wasn't over from Germany very long either. He couldn't even speak any English at all when he came over...During the first world war, he couldn't even speak English enough to have any services at all, and when the people got so hateful there about the German speaking, they made us close

that church so we sure did. We couldn't hardly have
any church, and since Becker was our pastor and he
couldn't speak English hardly at all, then we said we
wasn't going to give up everything, we was going to
have our little get-togethers in homes but we sure had
to keep that quiet, so nobody found out about that,
where we had our German church in the homes.
Then Pastor Becker went to Goldthwaite one day for
some reason and he couldn't speak very much English
and he had to speak German to some people in
Goldthwaite and that's when they tried to pick him up
for a spy and they liked to have really put him in jail
before he got out of Goldthwaite again. Some people
taken up for him and so he could get away from there
and he made a stop at Lawrences'... and when he
stopped there, he was so shaky and so tore up over
what he got into. Mrs. Lawrence didn't even have no
bread in the house, either, but she made him some
pancakes and he ate a bite and he made it home. No,
that really got to him, it really did, before he got out
of Goldthwaite. No, there were some German haters
at that time... Now Pastor Becker, after that he went
to college again and learned enough English so he
could have a little German service there and a little
English service that he could get by anyway...It was
pretty rough on him before he could speak enough
English to get by on. – *Annie Lippe*

Another upsetting experience was the invasion of Annie's
mother-in-law's home.

My mother-in-law had a picture in her house from
Kaiser Wilhelm. And we was all gone that Sunday,
and she and one of the children come home and that
picture was on the floor, tromped to pieces...We
wouldn't lock the doors out there on the farm at all. –
Annie Lippe

Shortages

Even in good times, there was barely enough food to support the large Lippe family, but during the wars, the shortages were even worse. Annie remembered,

> And then we wouldn't have flour to even make bread. All that stuff had to be shipped over to help and everything went down in the ocean. *(Many of the ships carrying supplies to the troops were sunk by German submarines)* And then you were allowed to eat so-and-so many meals a day. Now *(before the war)* in the morning we ate a snack in the field and another around ten o'clock in the evening. But three meals a day, that was all you was allowed, from breakfast and dinner and supper. Boy, if they would catch you eating through the window...they would call Goldthwaite pretty quick to say you ate an extra meal. No, like bread, now that was something a person needs, but we had cornmeal, but Joe Ann, that child just couldn't get that cornbread down. Then we could get Aunt Jemima pancakes. – *Annie Lippe*

Lena remembered the tough times during World War II.

> Everyone sacrificed things to help the cause. Ration books were distributed. We used them for sugar, shoes and other things. No one got nylon hose as it was needed for parachutes. The shoes I got married in were synthetic. They were also cheaper than leather shoes.
> As the brothers went to the service one by one, the girls had to help with more and more things. I never liked feed grinding and hog killing days. – *Lena Lippe Teinert*

During World War II everything was rationed. The Lippe family had their own meat, but Annie had trouble getting enough sugar to do her canning of peaches. Someone suggested that she use Karo corn syrup instead of sugar, which she did. Corn syrup was an important sugar substitute for early Texans, and many wonderful recipies still used today came from the substitution of corn syrup for sugar, most notably the Texas favorite, pecan pie.

9. Church, School, Fun Times, Mischief

Importance of religion

It was faith in God that sustained the Lippe family through many difficult times. Their beliefs and traditions were deeply rooted in the Lutheran Church going back to their homeland for generations, and God was their guide in every aspect of life.

Lydia once commented, "When we were little my Dad would read out of the Bible and sing a song after our meal at supper. I felt it wasn't right. Now that I'm older I think of my Dad how important it was all of us together at the table praising the Lord and singing. Thank you, Dad."

When the family bought a radio, the only program the children were allowed to listen to was "The Lutheran Hour," first broadcast in 1930. One day when their dad had gone into town, some of the children decided to tune the radio in the barn to another station. When he came home and caught them listening to secular music, they were in big trouble.

In 1941, the two Lutheran churches in Mills County united under the name of Zion Evangelical Lutheran Church. Gus and Sophie Bufe and Louise Lippe and family are pictured as founding families in the book commemorating the 100th anniversary of the churches.

Zion Lutheran Church, Priddy, Texas.

All of the children were baptized as babies and confirmed when they were about twelve. Sundays were reserved for attending church and socializing with friends and family, doing only the work that was absolutely necessary. Ruth said, "In 1940 when my family and I moved to Veribest, we attended Trinity Lutheran church in Miles, Texas where I was confirmed at the age of fifteen. I enjoyed church activities such as the choir, Luther League, and teaching Sunday School." All of the Lippe children remained active in church as they raised their own families.

When they lived on the Tiemann place, Fritz and Annie bought an organ. It was not working, but an uncle was able to repair it. Ben thought they bought it about 1936 and paid $15.00 for it. The organ was bought for Lydia to learn to play. She never learned to play well, but Katie did, and said, "I still have the books Lydia learned to play from. Ben remembers her practicing at night. I used those same music books to learn." Katie learned to play well enough to play the church organ for services. Martha and Lena also learned to play from the books, and Ruth learned to play "What a

Friend We Have in Jesus" from the books, although she said that she would much rather play by ear, just picking out the songs without looking at the notes.

Lippe family organ.

Church services were quite different in those days, as Annie recalled.

> I still have all these little German papers from when the children were in Sunday School. Instead of having hymnals in church, we had little songbooks, and each one had to have their songbook on Sunday morning. You had better not forget either, when you go to church and when they'd get confirmed, that was one gift they'd always get from their sponsors, a little songbook. I still have a whole bunch here in the organ...and church was different. Used to, all the

menfolks would have their one side and the ladies would have the other side. When that started mixing, I thought that really was not right at all. The menfolk didn't have no problem with the little children, though. That was the ladies' problem. – *Annie Lippe*

The importance of religion in the lives of the Lippe family was evident in Katie's words. Their faith in God was strong.

Through all this, looking back over 77 years, it is an awesome view. How God working through so many generations from Germany, through wars, boll weevils and whatnot, even with Dad's mental state he taught us the most important thing--to keep God the center of our lives--and Mama living it in her life. None of our family had college degrees and yet we all have had good lives, decent homes and food. To God be the glory. – *Katie Lippe Richards*

Celebrating birthdays and Christmas

Martha remembered,

Some of the ways we would celebrate birthdays were--all the Post Toasties (with milk and sugar) that we wanted to eat. At least that didn't require a lot of cooking--an easy meal that way.

And if we didn't have any watermelon in the garden Dad would go to town and buy one. He would put it in a tub of cold water and when it was nice and cold everyone would eat watermelon for the birthday meal. I never liked watermelon, so I would go out to the garden and try to find a nice ripe tomato, and that would be my special treat.

And sometimes we would make a gallon freezer of homemade ice cream for the special birthday meal. Kind of nice memories from growing up. – *Martha Lippe Hosum*

Here are some of Martin's memories of birthday celebrations:

> When one of the Lippe children had a birthday, they would find their plate upside down at the breakfast table with a small gift underneath, perhaps a pocket knife for the boys or a handkerchief for the girls.
>
> At the evening meal, their dad would come home from town with 3 giant economy sized boxes of Post Toasties as a special birthday treat. The family would eat all of them. Dried cereal was a special treat, because breakfast usually consisted of oatmeal or bacon and eggs. – *Martin Lippe*

Annie's earliest childhood memory is a Christmas Eve. After an early supper, the table was cleared and covered with their best white tablecloth; then each child turned his plate upside down. The children left the room, and Santa put a gift under each plate. Annie's gift was a coat with a silver lining bulging from underneath the plate. She recalled, "Christmas we all had to say a speech, Bible verse I think, before we opened gifts. The tree had candles on and we didn't see it until Christmas Eve. We always sang "Silent Night" in German."

Lena recalled,

> The Christmas tree was never put up until the afternoon of Christmas Eve. The main event was always the church Christmas Eve service and Christmas Day service.
>
> Sometimes it was hard to get up in front of the congregation and recite our piece. Mom always had lots of cakes and coffee cake at Christmas, and always coffee cake for Sunday morning breakfast. – *Lena Lippe Teinert*

Annie also told John Franklin about how the Christmas tree was a big event in their lives. The church was closed when they arrived, and they were not allowed to enter.

> We'd stay outside until everything was ready, Christmas tree lit and then the church opened. Boy, that was sure lit up. Then we had little sacks under the Christmas tree with little apples and candy in it. Some of them had little gifts. No, that was not like it is now. – *Annie Lippe*

So, you might ask, how did they have lights on the church Christmas tree in the days before electricity and strings of electric light bulbs? The answer is somewhat horrifying to us living today with all of our safety rules and regulations! Annie's answer?

> Just candles. And then they had a long stick and it had a little cotton on it and in case those candles would catch fire, they wet it right quick so it wouldn't spread on the Christmas tree. They'd stand behind the tree, some of the trustees, what they called the elders, and they had that little cotton on it and a little water and they'd dip it in and then...so the candle wouldn't spread the fire on the Christmas tree. Those wax candles would drip and start burning where they'd start dripping, too. That was a big celebration at Christmas time. Everything was closed until they were ready to start. They'd open that door wide and then we would walk in. Boy, that was bright lights in front of your eyes. We had a little Christmas tree in the house every year, too, with little candles. – *Annie Lippe*

Yes, they also had a tree in their home covered with lit candles! Annie said, "But that was kinda dangerous. If a person wouldn't watch it real close the cedar would catch fire and cedar, that burns, I'll tell you, and it goes into flames pretty quick." What a scary thought, having real candles on a Christmas tree!

Farming takes priority over school

Neither Fritz nor Annie's mothers knew how to speak English, although their fathers did. When Annie started school, they were taught for half of the day in German and the other half in English. When some of her older children started school, they could speak only German and were taught in English, so it was very hard for them at first. On Lydia's first day of school, the teacher handed her a book and a pair of scissors. Not knowing any English, she decided that her job was to cut pictures out of the book, which was not at all what the teacher intended! Velma said,

> We are of the German race and had been speaking German until we were in school. There we were required to speak English. One day we were playing with our dolls when our Dad asked us not to talk German. So while playing we talked very little. –
> *Velma Lippe Bretting*

Annie, like many others of that era, only made it through about the fourth grade in school, attending only when she was not needed to work in the field. She said, "I can read and write, but I never could figure. I still have to have help with that."

On the first day of school, all of the children would get their books and would not return for six weeks because they were needed on the farm to pick cotton. The teacher would pick up the children and take them to the one-room school house to teach the basic reading, writing, arithmetic, geography, history, and if one got far enough in school, algebra. Joe Ann cried when her father told her that she would have to quit school in the seventh grade but she continued to study on her own from any books that were available. Because of the demands of the farm, most of the Lippe children were not able to stay in school long enough to graduate, although most were able to graduate later or acquire vocational training.

Ready for school, Meyer farm, about 1940.
Ruth, age 9; Martin, 11; Ben, 15; Lena, 14; Katie, 10.

Fun times

This was taken from another school paper by Martin's granddaughter Sarah from a conversation with her grandfather:

> It was a time when vacations were unimaginable because even going fishing with the family provided guilt when other things could be done, so his mother brought all the clothes that needed to be patched and patched them all afternoon. Holidays were spent going to church and then working on the farm because there was too much to be done to waste one day. Church was the social gathering and games were invented at home, except for Christmas when a volleyball net and volleyball were given to all the kids because there were enough for practically two teams! – *Sarah Lippe*

Lena said, "Sunday afternoons were usually spent visiting friends and relatives." She also remembered some of the games they played.

> With no T.V. or computer we entertained ourselves with baseball, kick the can, andy over, marbles, jacks and other games. Later we got a volley ball. That was fun. – *Lena Lippe Teinert*

Martin said that they swam at the Bryant Farm where there was a nice pool of water to swim in.

> Often after church you would gather in someone's home for a big meal. Men would eat first, then the women and finally the children. After dinner the men would play dominoes or 42, pitch washers and horseshoes, play croquet, and often one could hear a lively discussion or argument, perhaps on a subject of the Bible. The women did the cooking, dishwashing, tended the babies, discussed sewing, canning, quilting and children, etc. The children loved playing with their cousins and friends. *-From This Is Your Life, compiled for Annie's 90th birthday by Dora Steinmann Lippe*

Mischief

Yes, even these hardworking, strictly disciplined farm children sometimes got into a bit of mischief. It was on the Schuster farm where Lydia, around age seven or eight, and her brother John, a year younger, noticed a field where the plants looked a little uneven. They decided that the field would look better if they would lie down in it and roll around until all of the plants were flat. She did not remember what crop it was, but it was one of the feed crops for livestock and her dad was just about ready to harvest it. Their dad was very angry when he saw what they had done, and John got a terrible spanking. Lydia said that she was spanked, too, but not as much as John.

Martin told a tale of a misadventure with his older brother Ben, recorded by Martin's granddaughter, Sarah.

> After answering all the basic questions about the lifestyle during this period, memories were refreshed and stories were remembered. Grandpa's first story is that of when he was about seven and his older brother Ben was about ten, it was a Sunday and the family was planning on going and visiting some neighbors. The two boys did not want to go because they had already made plans on what they were going to do while the family was out. Their parents were at first hesitant but reluctantly agreed to let them stay home. The boys had been secretly planning to crank the 1929 Chevrolet truck. After the family had left the boys went out to the truck and Martin was in charge of retarding or advancing the spark in the truck while Ben was going to physically crank the truck outside to start it. Ben told Martin what levers to move and not move, but Martin did not do so as planned allowing the engine to backfire, breaking Ben's right arm. The Schulze family was not far away and so the boys went inside to call. Ben could not call because the handle was on the right side, so Martin stood on a chair and turned the handle to make the correct ring pattern for the Schulzes while Ben did the talking. The neighbor children where the parents were heard the ring and picked up the phone listening to the party line, they told Martin and Ben's parents who came and took Ben to the hospital. Their dad just bought insurance and so he believed the trip would not cost them a dime, but the insurance was soon dropped after only about six months because it would not cover the charge since Ben did not stay overnight in the hospital. – *Sarah Lippe interview with her grandfather, Martin Lippe*

10. Illnesses, Accidents, Miraculous Escapes

In rearing a family of eleven children on a farm, there were many injuries and accidents, some minor, and some which could have resulted in serious injury or death. It is truly amazing that eleven of Fritz and Annie's twelve children survived to adulthood. The only one who did not was little Annie, who died soon after she was born.

Joe Ann had a frightening experience while using a horse-drawn cultivator at the Schuster farm. The harness became tangled and the horses kept backing up until they went over the bank and into the creek, with Joe Ann still hanging on. Lydia was watching when her sister and the horses disappeared over the edge of the cliff. Fortunately, Joe Ann was not injured. Lydia was also right behind Joe Ann when she came upon a rattlesnake with babies in a row of cotton they were picking.

Joe Ann was often the doctor and nurse for her younger siblings and substitute mother when Annie was ill. Martin was a small boy when he found a piece of glass on the ground, picked it up and swallowed it. They attempted to contact the doctor, but Joe Ann decided that would take too long, so she reached into Martin's throat and pulled out the glass. Joe Ann herself was injured when she fell down stairs carrying two jars of peaches. The jars broke and the glass cut her wrists severely.

Lydia remembered two things that happened to her at the Stegemoller place. One was a bad fall. She was riding with her father on a wagon load of hay to open gates for him and keep the livestock from getting out while he drove the wagon through. The wagon passed under a wire that was just the right height to catch Lydia under the chin and knock her backward off the wagon onto the ground. Her back never completely recovered.

Lydia also nearly lost a hand when they lived at the Stegemoller place. She had a blister on her hand from using a hoe, and it became badly infected. Her parents took her to the doctor, who told them that he would have to amputate the hand to save her life. Annie refused and said that they would see another doctor first.

The second doctor looked carefully at her hand and said that he might be able to save it by performing surgery. Lydia had overheard her parents talk to the doctor about amputating her hand, so when she awoke from surgery, she asked for her hand. Her mother did not understand what she meant, but the nurse did, and carefully pulled back the bandage to show Lydia that she still had her hand and all of her fingers. Lydia said that she had thanked God a thousand times for saving her hand.

Annie and Fritz were living on the Bryant farm when they almost lost their daughter Martha due to a ruptured appendix. She was in Scott & White Hospital in Temple for almost two months, and she did not get out of bed to walk one single step for the entire time. She was not allowed to eat anything for almost three weeks, and lost 29 pounds while in the hospital. Her mother stayed with her much of the time, reading devotions and praying. Martha came home two days before her seventeenth birthday, but became ill again and had to return to the hospital for about two more weeks. She had been in bed for so long that she had to learn to walk all over again.

Ben was very young when they lived on the Schuster farm, but he remembered his narrow escape from a rattlesnake bite.

> My experience with the rattlesnake occurred when I was about three years old. Dad told me to crawl under the barn and gather the eggs the chickens had laid. Now, a miracle is just about to be told. When I was about three feet from the egg nest the rattlesnake raised its ugly head, rattled his tongue at me and just about to strike. I didn't just shout for Dad. I screamed at the top of my lungs, "There's a snake in the egg nest." Dad said, "Come out from under the barn, now." I was very happy and eager to obey. Dad immediately went into the house, got his shotgun and killed the rattlesnake. If I had gotten any closer to the egg nest the snake would have struck me in the face and I would not be writing this letter. On that day, God protected me from harm.

A few years later, we kids were playing in the barn. To my amazement, I found a very pretty spider. The little creature was so enticing I begin to play with it. Soon, the pretty black widow spider was crawling on my hand. After a while it bit me on my thumb and the pretty little spider was not so pretty any more. I ran into the house crying and mommy immediately tried to doctor it. It did no good. The bite was having a terrible effect making me very sick. They took me to the doctor but by then the venom had stopped working. Thank God for protecting me. – *Ben Lippe*

Ben also told the story of a buggy accident when the Lippe family truly had a miraculous escape from injury or death. They were living on the Bryant farm at the time.

The third thing happened when we went to a cousin's wedding. The only transportation our family had was a horse and buggy. We went to the wedding and later to her house for the reception. There was a lot of food, visiting and laughing with the kinfolks and us kids romping and playing just having good old fashioned fun. By the time we started back to the house, it was getting dark and the road was not paved. We met a car going the other way and a cloud of dust covered us all, getting into our eyes and lungs. Not too long after that, another car was coming fast up behind us. He did not see us in the buggy until it was too late. The man swerved trying to miss us but it was unavoidable. He hit the left rear wheel of the buggy and we jolted to a sudden stop. At this time another miracle transpired, thank God. The horse did not try to run and he was not hurt. I don't know just who all were in the buggy but none of us were injured. We thanked God for his protection. However, the driver of the car was not as fortunate as we were. The driver's leg was badly injured and he

walked with a limp for the rest of his life.
Fortunately, he did not hit the buggy full force, or the
occupants probably would not have survived. The
buggy was totally demolished. After that incident,
our father decided to get our family's first car—a
1935 Chevrolet pickup. – *Ben Lippe*

Martin told the story of his tuberculosis diagnosis and his
treatment and recovery at a sanitarium for nine months, which
probably saved his life and turned out to be a much better
experience than anyone could have hoped for. *(A sanitarium was a
health resort where people with tuberculosis and other diseases
were sent to recover. Patients were often kept in isolation to
prevent the spread of disease.)* It may have been the equivalent of
going to a summer camp for this hardworking farm boy, with
emphasis placed on rest and a healthy diet.

In March of 1942, at the age of 13, I was
given a skin test to determine if I was infected with
tuberculosis. The skin test was positive and x-rays
confirmed I had active tuberculosis. I was admitted
to the Texas State Tuberculosis Sanitarium in
Carlsbad, Texas on March 28th.
There are a few unhappy memories, but most
important there are a lot of happy memories. Being
away from home for an extended time was difficult
for about three weeks. After that life was very
pleasant. There were about seventy boys in four
wards, so there was always something going on. We
were allowed to have visitors two hours Sunday
afternoons. Young children were not allowed on the
playground of the children's hospital. So Katie and
Ruth *(ages 12 and 11)* were required to stay in the
parking lot, and talk to me across the street, while I
visited with parents and other family members.
The treatment at the time was a very rigid
schedule with a lot of time for rest and a very healthy
diet. We were required to eat everything that was on

our tray, even if there was something we did not like. The only thing I could not eat was boiled asparagus. When a nurse was not looking, I would put it under the plate on my tray, and somehow I always got by with that.

We attended school all summer, except two weeks which gave the teachers time for their vacations.

We were involved in a Boy Scout Troop. The meetings were scheduled Saturday mornings, and if the weather was good we would have an outing at the Concho River, which was approximately one mile from the Sanitarium.

The nurses were very pleasant, and they maintained good discipline. Mrs. Brown was very special. She enjoyed working with the boys, and all the boys liked her. She worked in the children's hospital while her husband was a patient at the Sanitarium. Before the lights were turned off at 9:00 PM, she would have all the boys kneel at the foot end of the beds, and lead us in saying this prayer, then kiss each one "Good night."

> Now I lay me down to sleep.
> I pray the Lord my soul to keep.
> If I should die before I wake,
> I pray the Lord my soul to take.
> If I should live for other days,
> I pray the Lord to guide my ways.

We went to a movie each Thursday night. If a boy caused trouble, he was not allowed to go to the movie. He was required to go to bed at 7:00 o'clock.

We were required to stay at the Sanitarium nine months, which meant that I would be released December 28th. I was released the week end before Christmas, which was a few days less than nine months.

Conner, Joe Ann, and my parents took me home in Conner and Joe Ann's car, because their car had a heater, which our 1937 Ford did not have.

I think about that time of my life often, and am thankful that God provided everything I needed at that critical time. – *Martin Lippe*

Martin at Carlsbad Sanatarium.

Lena visiting Martin at Carlsbad.

Annie's recovery from the brink of death after complications arose after giving birth to her 12th child was probably the most miraculous of all, surprising everyone, especially the doctor. From "This Is Your Life," compiled for Annie's 95th birthday by Dora Steinmann Lippe:

> Ruth was a baby when you had major surgery at Hamilton. The doctors said there was no way you could live. The doctor was gone for several days, and after he returned he was walking down the corridor and glanced in the room and saw you and said, "You still here?" He was so surprised he couldn't believe it.

It seems that God had other plans for her.

11. Children leaving the Nest

As soon as each of the Lippe children reached the age of eighteen, they were expected to move out and earn a living for themselves. Fritz gave them some help in getting started when they left home. He gave each daughter the money from the sale of the next calf born on the farm, and each son received twenty acres of cotton from the farm.

The older girls found jobs in housekeeping, either for individuals or in hotels. Joe Ann and Lydia worked together at the Atkinson Hotel in Hamilton, for a weekly salary of $13. They worked in the dining room at mealtime, and also cleaned rooms, washed the sheets, and ironed them in a steam press until Mrs. Atkinson finally decided that the sheets did not need to be ironed. Velma and Lena also worked as housekeepers, as did Katie, until she found a job as a nurse's aid, then as a dental assistant. Ruth worked in a cafeteria and a drugstore before she was offered a job at Texas Electric Service Company, where she worked for many years.

Joe Ann and friends at work.

Ruth and Katie in work uniforms.

San Angelo street scene during World War II.

All four sons served in the army, John and Fritz during World War II, Ben with the occupation forces in Japan after the war, and Martin, who was drafted just before the end of the Korean war. All of the men the daughters married also served in the military, several in combat areas. The end of World War II was a joyful time and it was a great relief to Annie that her boys made it home safely.

John in uniform, World War II.

Fritz in uniform, World War II.

Ben in uniform, just after World War II.

Martin in uniform, just after Korean war.

Lippe family, San Angelo, May 29, 1943. John and Fritz were home on leave during World War II. Back row (standing): Velma, age 21; Lena, 16; Fritz, 23; Joe Ann, 31; Lydia, 27; John, 26; Ben, 18; Martha, 19. Front (seated): Martin, 14; Katie, 13; Papa Fritz, 57; Annie, 54; Ruth, 11.

After the war ended, jobs in West Texas were becoming plentiful due to the oil boom, and several of Annie's grown children settled in the Odessa and Midland areas. All of the sons found good careers in their chosen fields. Two daughters, Lydia and Martha, married "Yankees" and moved to Minnesota, and Martin found his sweetheart in Missouri while he was stationed there. Each one of Annie's children found a wonderful spouse who was loved by her and by the rest of the family. All remained active in their churches and carried their faith into the rearing of their families, giving Annie a total of 29 grandchildren and, as of this writing, the number of great-grandchildren is approaching 100.

12. *Annie's Later Years*

In 1952, Annie and her two youngest children, Martin and Ruth, moved to a home at 802 North Kelly, in Odessa. Ruth said that when they moved to Odessa, it was the first time she lived in a house with a phone, running water, and a bathroom with all the facilities. She said, "What luxury!" Annie lived in that house for forty of her 103-1/2 years, much longer than she lived anywhere else. With the help of her children and the rent from a tiny apartment on the back of the lot, she was able to pay off the mortgage and finally have a home that was her very own.

Annie's home in Odessa, soon after she bought the house in 1952.

A few of Annie's older grandchildren remember her last farm house, but they were very young and their memories are vague. All of her grandchildren have wonderful memories of holidays spent at her house in Odessa and the coffeecake she made when she expected visitors. Her home was often the center of the family's Thanksgiving and Christmas celebrations.

Annie had many rewards for her years of hard work as the mother of eleven children on a farm. Her children helped her financially and repaired her home when needed. They also took her on trips as long as she was able to ride in a car for long periods of time. She made several trips to Minnesota and Missouri, the first of which was by train, the others by automobile, but none by airplane. The out-of-state children and their families came to visit her many times also.

Annie standing beside the altar in Bethlehem Lutheran Church, Washington County, where she was confirmed.

Annie's son John and his wife, Dora, took her to Washington County in 1974, to see the places where she had lived as a child, and relatives she had not seen in years. She even rode the ferry and spent the night on Galveston Island, something she said she would never do. At Galveston, in spite of her fear of the water, she summoned the courage to stand at the edge of the Gulf of Mexico, thinking of her parents who crossed the ocean.

Annie at the water's edge, Galveston, 1974.

For many years, Fritz's mental illness had made him a danger to himself and his family. After all attempts to help him failed, he was committed to San Antonio State Hospital in 1948. His children and grandchildren visited often, sometimes bringing Annie along and taking him out for lunch on a day pass.

Annie and Fritz Lippe, 50th Anniversary, December 10, 1960.

In 1958, Fritz was transferred to Kerrville State Hospital, where he and Annie observed their 50th wedding anniversary in 1960. Ben drove his mother to Kerrville, where they had their picture taken by a photographer. After three years in Kerrville, Fritz became ill with a gland and kidney infection. He was moved back to San Antonio in 1961 for surgery, but his heart became too weak for the operation. **Fritz H. Lippe died** in San Antonio State Hospital on **June 20, 1961**, at the age of 75 years.

Annie's family and friends gathered to celebrate her birthday at ages 90, 95, and 100 years. With the help of her children, Annie was able to live in her own home until age 99, when she made the decision to move to a nursing home. She visited several and chose a new Lutheran facility, The Parks Good Samaritan Home, in Odessa, and moved there on December 9, 1987. She celebrated her 100th birthday there, with her nine living children and many grandchildren and great-grandchildren present.

Annie with her children on her 100th birthday, 1988.
Back row: Martin, Lena, Velma, Ruth, John;
Front row: Martha, Katie, Lydia, Ben; Seated: Annie, born August 28, 1888.
Missing were Joe Ann, who died in 1975, and Fritz, who died in 1985.

Annie with 16 of her 29 grandchildren
on her 100th birthday, 1988. Back row: Larry, Johnny, Donna, Dennis (partly hidden), and Mark; Middle: Mike, Tracy, Sharon, Gloria, Byron, Dan, Phyllis, Charlotte, Julie; Front: Gwen and Susan kneeling beside Annie.

Annie with many of her great-grandchildren on her 100th birthday, 1988.
The numbers continue to grow, and her descendants are spread across the
United States at the time of this writing.

Annie was visited often by her children and grandchildren
who lived in Odessa, and as often as possible by those who lived at a
greater distance. Katie went to the nursing home almost every night
to tuck her mother in, as her mother had done for her as a child.
Katie wrote, "This is the prayer I would read Mama almost every
night before tucking her in at the nursing home. This prayer, and
Psalm 100."

Annie Lippe's Favorite Evening Prayer

Now the light has gone away;
Father, listen while I pray,
Asking Thee to watch and keep
And to send me quiet sleep.

Jesus, Savior, wash away
All that has been wrong today;
Help me every day to be
Good and gentle, more like Thee.

Let my near and dear ones be
Always near and dear to Thee;

Oh, bring me and all I love
To Thy happy home above.

Now my evening praise I give;
Thou didst die that I might live.
All my blessings come from Thee;
Oh, how good Thou art to me!

Thou, my best and kindest Friend,
Thou wilt love me to the end.
Let me love Thee more and more,
Always better than before.

Psalm 100, RSV

1. Make a joyful noise to the Lord, all
the lands!
2. Serve the Lord with gladness!
Come into His presence with singing!
3. Know that the Lord is God! It is He
that made us, and we are His, we are
His people, and the sheep of His
pasture.
4. Enter His gates with thanksgiving,
and His courts with praise! Give
thanks to Him, bless His name!
5. For the Lord is good; His steadfast
love endures forever, and His
faithfulness to all generations.

Annie Bufe Lippe died on February 21, 1992. In addition to little Annie, who died soon after birth, two other children predeceased her—daughter Joe Ann in 1975, and son Fritz in 1985. One of her children who lived nearby was always with their mother near the end. Lena and Ruth had been with her earlier in the day. Ruth said,

Ben was the only one with Mama when she died. We were taking turns staying with her. I had spent most of the afternoon with her. When Ben came, I went home. I had just gotten home when Ben called and said she passed away. – *Ruth Lippe Atkins Cleckler*

Annie is buried beside her husband Fritz in Sunset Memorial Gardens, Odessa, Texas. She left a wonderful legacy, and my wish in writing this book is that her descendants will learn about her and appreciate her struggles to survive and make life better for her children, grandchildren and great-grandchildren.

Annie Bufe Lippe at age 101.
Her sweet smile will never be forgotten.

CHILDREN AND GRANDCHILDREN OF
ANNIE AND FRITZ LIPPE

Joe Ann Lippe, born October 29, 1911, married Conner W. Gholson on October 1, 1938. One daughter, Donna Ann, born February 26, 1945.

Lydia Louise Lippe, born February 16, 1916, married Arnold W. Schlueter, Sr. on October 15, 1943. Four sons: Arnold Lynn, Jr., born September 7, 1945; Allan Wayne, born September 11, 1948; Jerry Lee, born October 27, 1954; and Kevin Dale, born July 24, 1958.

John A. Lippe, born June 29, 1917, married Dora Mae Steinmann on July 15, 1943. Three sons: Johnny Ray, born June 21, 1945; Larry Glen, born December 4, 1947; and Kenneth Royce, born July 3, 1952.

Fritz Adolph Lippe, born March 18, 1920, married Lillie Ruth Burleson on November 22, 1946. Three children: Shirley Marie, born March 3, 1948; Michael Wayne, born January 27, 1950; and Frederick Norman, born January 27, 1956.

Velma Anna Lippe, born September 17, 1921, married Edlin K. Bretting on March 10, 1945. Three children: Gloria Mae, born June 7, 1946; Dennis James, born September 3, 1950; and Mary Joyce, born May 15, 1953.

Martha Hilda Lippe, born September 21, 1923, married Gerhard "Gary" K. Hosum on March 5, 1948. Two children (adopted): Ronald Kenneth, born January 1, 1954; and Janet Marie, born May 14, 1959.

Benjamin Henry Lippe, born March 13, 1925, married Lillie Rose Meissner on December 29, 1950. Four children: Daniel Lee, born January 18, 1952; Charlotte Ann, born April 29, 1954; Phyllis Kay, born February 28, 1959; and Byron Dale, born June 19, 1960.

Magdalena Emma "Lena" Lippe, born October 12, 1926, married Emil B. Teinert on August 16, 1949. Three children: John Earl, born June 4, 1950; Sharon Kay, born July 21, 1952; and Elaine Susan, born July 31, 1955.

Martin William Lippe, born February 25, 1929, married Elsie Louise Hinck on February 5, 1955. Two sons: Mark Gregory, born April 26, 1958; and David Keith, born March 13, 1963.

Katie Frieda Lippe, born May 4, 1930, married William "Bill" Richards on May 14, 1955. Four daughters: Carla Dawn, born November 18, 1958; Gwen Marie, born August 18, 1960; Tracy Lynne, born February 15, 1962; and Julie Ann, born October 21, 1963.

Ruth Minnie Lippe, born September 16, 1931, married (1st) Royce Leon Atkins on May 29, 1969, and she enjoyed spending time with her four stepchildren, Roy, Kay, Debbie, and Mike Atkins. Leon died in a tragic auto accident on February 13, 1989, and ten years later, Ruth married (2nd) John C. Cleckler on January 1, 1999, and added two more stepchildren to her family, John's daughters Connie and Christina.

Many great-grandchildren and great-great-grandchildren have been added to Annie's descendants. Some of those listed above have passed away.

For many more Lippe family stories and photos, with complete references and index, please refer to my 2009 book, *Fritz and Annie Lippe Family, German Cotton Farmers in Early 1900s Texas*, available through major booksellers. For more information, see my website, www.gholson-cook.com

Donna Gholson Cook

ABOOKS

ALIVE Book Publishing and ALIVE Publishing Group
are imprints of Advanced Publishing LLC,
3200 A Danville Blvd., Suite 204, Alamo, California 94507

Telephone: 925.837.7303 Fax: 925.837.6951
www.alivebookpublishing.com

www.ingramcontent.com/pod-product-compliance
Lightning Source LLC
Chambersburg PA
CBHW030510100426
42813CB00002B/422